Daisy's Story

Wynter Sommers

Registered With
UK Copyright Service   UK © CS
Reg. No.: 284721054

This work is registered with the UK Copyright Service, in accordance with the Copyright, Designs and Patents Act 1988. All rights reserved 284721054

USA Copyright © 2017 Susan E dePillis and GJ dePillis

TXu 2 - 058 – 391 and TXu 705 – 664

Library of Congress Control Number: 2018943515

PURE FORCE
ENTERPRISES INC

Published by Pure Force Enterprises, Inc.
California, USA
Since 2002

INGRAM
INGRAM® Distribution

All rights reserved. No part of this book may be used or reproduced by any means, graphic, electronic, or mechanical, including photocopying, recording, taping or by any information storage retrieval system without the written permission of the authors except in the case of brief quotations embodied in critical articles and reviews.

This novel is a work of fiction. Names, places, characters, and incidents are either the product of the author's imagination or, if real, are used fictitiously.

ISBN-13: 978-0-9791080-1-3
ISBN-10: 0-9791080-1-2

DEDICATION

To all of us who yearn to be in a loving, trusting family so we may not only dream of a better tomorrow but build a peaceful future.

DAISY'S ADVENTURES

1 DAISY'S STORY

2 DAISY'S INDEPENDENCE DAY PICNIC

3 DAISY'S SPECIAL DATE

4 DAISY'S HOMEWORK

5 DAISY'S PARROT

6 DAISY AND THE GERRY

7 DAISY AND THE FACTS

8 DAISY'S ICE CREAM GARDEN

9 DAISY'S WHITE HOUSE

CONTENTS

1 CHAPTER 1

2 CHAPTER 12

3 CHAPTER 25

4 CHAPTER 30

5 CHAPTER 36

6 CHAPTER 47

7 CHAPTER 53

ACKNOWLEDGMENTS

To all those who have been selfless givers of considerations and who dole out tokens of love to provide hope.

1 CHAPTER

Miss Smithy happily scooped full ladles of steaming, freshly prepared, oatmeal into each child's breakfast bowl. Twenty-four children sat around the long breakfast table.

Noticing not all the seats were filled, Miss Smithy called out, "I need every child in their seats, so we have time to clean up before your forever families come to meet you!"

Just then a little girl raced into the dining hall as several children buzzed with excitement about the prospects of meeting their future forever families.

Miss Smithy said, "Daisy! You nearly missed a hot breakfast. You will need your strength to clean up in time before Mrs. Young opens the doors this morning. After the years you've lived here, you know our Trustees and Governing Board only allow us to set up child-parent matches once a month."

"Yes," Daisy skidded to a halt, out of breath. She held the basket of eggs she had just collected from the chicken coop outside. Daisy placed the basket on the sideboard. "Our future parents don't come as much because we are at war. I remember."

Cook came out of the kitchen and smiled at Daisy. She picked up the basket, held up an egg to the light and nodded. Then she blew on each egg as she headed back to the kitchen. Small downy feathers floated off each egg as Cook walked away.

Miss Smithy asked, "What took you so…"

Daisy slipped into her seat with practiced ease. She explained to Miss Smithy, "Before I collected the eggs, Cook gave me a new jar of honey for breakfast…" Daisy giggled as she pointed to the sideboard, "I put the honey over there. Besides, I wanted to gather eggs for our dinner tonight."

Mrs. Young, sitting at the other end of the table asked Miss Smithy, "I thought you went into town and spoke to the butcher about dinner…"

Minnie, Daisy's friend asked, "Miss Smithy, are we going to have meat tonight?"

Daisy answered Minnie, "Don't be silly. Meat is rationed. What American needs meat when we have chickens to give us eggs. That's why I feed them as part of my chores."

Miss Smithy smiled, "Actually, Daisy, the butcher knew I was saving up our ration coupons and he will deliver a fine cut of meat later today. Cook already said she will make us a stew for dinner tonight to celebrate Company Day."

Mrs. Young smiled and asked Miss Smithy, "Did the butcher have any news…about the war? Is America winning? Or will we be invaded by those…those…"

Miss Smithy cut off Mrs. Young before she said anything which would upset the children, saying, "I'll share the newspaper later. It's only about a week old, so it gives us the most current news we can get way out here."

Mrs. Young said, "The Great War, which ended in 1918 was supposed to be the war which ended all wars. I cannot believe we are in a second war so soon after…and fighting the same enemy!"

Mrs. Young took the jar Daisy had placed on the side-board table and used a spoon to scoop out a dollop of amber honey into her own steaming bowl of hot oatmeal. She then passed the jar to the child next to her. He took some honey and passed the jar and spoon down the line to the girl seated next to him... and then to the next child and so on, to each child seated around the table.

Daisy raised her hand, "Miss Smithy, can we read the funnies from the newspaper you got from the butcher?"

Miss Smithy smiled, "Of course, Daisy. After Mrs. Young notes the Bide-A-While Children's Log Book at the end of today to see which of the families you liked."

Minnie piped up, "Sometimes I feel as if they are shopping for children and we don't have a choice."

Mrs. Young shook her head, "Not here at Bide-A-While, Minnie. Here we listen to you. Even if the prospective parents like you...if you do not like them, it is not a match. We need both the child and the family to agree that it is a good match. That is why we keep the log book current."

Daisy scooped honey into her hot oatmeal and then ran her fingers through her tangled locks, "I guess we have to look our best?"

Minnie whispered to Daisy, "I have a comb and an extra hair ribbon if you want to borrow it after breakfast before the doors open to let the grown-ups in."

Daisy asked the two teachers, "If the war ended today, would we all get forever families today?"

Miss Smithy and Mrs. Young looked at each other, then at Daisy as Mrs. Young explained, "The war slows down the process for sure, Daisy. But God has a wonderful plan for each of you. Be patient."

Daisy crinkled her nose, "It's just... Is it my hair? I feel like I've been here so long and...no family has taken me in, yet."

Cook popped her head out of the kitchen, "Daisy," Cook announced, "These eggs are lovely. I am so thankful you have a way with those birds. Since Butcher is delivering meat later on, could I ask you to fetch some onions and carrots from the garden?"

Daisy smiled, "Of course, Cook. I was going to scoop some of the chicken droppings into the compost heap to fertilize the garden later today, anyway. I can get those veggies after the grown-ups leave."

Cook smiled at Mrs. Young and said, "Daisy is such a blessing here."

Mrs. Young looked at Daisy, "I can get those vegetables, Daisy. Why don't you let Minnie fix your hair and make sure your bed is made? Take time to look your best."

As the children chatted noisily amongst themselves, Daisy continued to converse with Mrs. Young, "So... How I look is why I have not been adopted?"

Mrs. Young shook her head, "Heavens no, Daisy. You look lovely. You are a real blessing to us, as Cook just said. Any family would be lucky to call you their own."

Mrs. Young looked around the table at each child and cleared her throat to speak over the chatter, "I would like to remind everybody to look their best and behave their best when they meet the grown-ups. When I set up the matches, I pray that God shows me the plan which He has for each and every one of you."

Bide-A-While orphanage was located high on a green knoll overlooking a sparkling river. The converted mansion nestled amongst rolling hills on a thick carpet of lush grasses. A gentle breeze whispered through the leaves of surrounding trees. This serene setting, far away from the bustling crowded city, was ideal for prospective parents to visit the children.

Daisy wondered if the setting was enough to encourage a maybe-family to be matched with her and perhaps even consider adopting her one day.

Miss Smithy bowed her head.

Bowing their heads as well, all the children now looked down at their delicious steaming bowls of honey-sweetened oatmeal. Miss Smithy prayed, "Oh Loving God, in the Name of Your Son, our Savior, we thank You for the food you have provided to all of us here at our Bide-A-While Children's Home. We thank You, also, for protecting us in America during this terrible war. We accept Your gracious guidance as you bless each of us. Amen."

Miss Smithy looked at her own bowl of porridge and then set the example by taking her napkin and placing it on her lap.

The children mimicked her action, placing napkins on their own laps.

Only when she smiled and said, "To your health and to God revealing your future forever-parents to you today, on Company Day... Bon Appetite..." did Miss Smithy take a bite of oatmeal.

Next, Mrs. Young took a spoonful of oatmeal as the children watched. Now that the two adults at the table had started eating, the children began eating their breakfasts, as well.

The orphans chatted excitedly about either meeting grown-ups for the first time or, for some, the second or third visit on this monthly Company Day.

Daisy smiled.

Miss Smithy had known Daisy since she was in Primaries. Miss Smithy was a fun-loving hopeful woman, who chased Daisy's fears and heartache away with a reminder of how God had a plan for her. It may not be an easy path, but it would be something custom-made just for Daisy. Miss Smithy always banished doubt as easily as an ostrich feather duster poofed away dust bunnies from underneath the beds.

A ray of sunshine brightened the morning fog, beaming through the window right onto Miss Smithy.

Her laughter mended hearts, broken in a time torn by the strife of WWII, hearts of both parents and children seeking forever-families, yearning to embrace a peaceful tomorrow together.

2 CHAPTER

After breakfast, Daisy made sure to look at herself in the mirror and smooth out any stray hairs. She also took a deep breath and made her bed properly.

She told herself that she would make a real effort to be tidy. She would show her future parents how neat her bed was. Just last week, Miss Smithy had shown her a special way to tuck in her sheets neatly. She called the technique "hospital corners" because, as a former nurse during the first Great War, she had to change the sheets a lot on patients' hospital beds.

Daisy was glad Miss Smithy kindly shared these little tricks. As Miss Smithy explained, these tasks are what a daughter would do in a future family. Daisy felt all the Bide-A-While etiquette was the sort of training she'd expect from parents, but...for now, Miss Smithy's guidance was preparing Daisy to take her place in a family setting.

Daisy walked outside and looked up. The morning sun streamed through leafy trees, casting misty beams of light into lacy patterns on the chicken coop. Daisy loved being outside. She often wondered that if her future parents were city-dwellers, would she be happy?

A lot of the prospective parents seemed to be from the city, but Daisy hoped for a mother and father who would take her camping and teach her about the stars in the sky.

Daisy grabbed a rake and began combing the ground to clean up the chicken coop. Next, she rested the rake against the side of the coop and gathered up some dried corn harvested from the Bide-A-While Victory gardens.

Then she fed breakfast to the chickens.

This was a chore she did with a smile, often giggling to herself as the wild birds, flying above, would greedily eye the feed given to the chickens. Daisy knew it was best that she remain for a few minutes to make sure the chickens did not have to fight those other birds for their breakfast.

Daisy moved the rake from the coop back to where it belonged with other garden tools, which were all resting against a lush ivy lattice frame beside a brick wall. She noted the time and realized she needed to wash up again.

"Daisy! Daisy! Oh," Mrs. Young said in surprise as she spied Daisy coming inside brushing her hands on her skirt. "Daisy, I was taking roll-call and you were missing... I told you I would collect the vegetables from the garden. You've got to get cleaned up!"

"The chickens needed breakfast," Daisy shrugged.

Mrs. Young rested her hands on each of Daisy's shoulders and said, "All the other children want to meet the grown-ups visiting today. Don't you want to be with them when we open the doors?"

Daisy just shrugged and looked down.

"Now, now, Daisy," Mrs. Young said in soft comforting tones, "Please don't act as if you don't care."

Daisy replied, "Sure, I care. It's just…"

"Just what, Daisy…" Mrs. Young urged.

"It's just that Minnie…" Daisy trailed off.

"Yes," Mrs. Young said, "Your best friend Minnie…"

Daisy sighed, shrugging yet again, and said, "Last month Minnie said she really liked the couple who came by and they are coming back today to see her, again.

I'm pretty sure they'll want to adopt her…and then I'll be alone."

"Daisy, let me tell you something…"

"What…"

"God has a plan for each of us. Miss Smithy used to be a nurse and helped a lot of soldiers in the first Great War to end all wars…which did not end them. I know this second war has caused a lot of grief in the world, but you need to focus on God's future which is customized just for you and your talents. Do not focus on Minnie leaving. We don't know if Minnie will get adopted or not. She also has a path God has tailored just for her, and you need to let her follow that path."

Daisy replied with frustration, "It's just that I have attended the Company Saturday over and over. I've said good-bye to Henry, Helen, Anna, Melissa, Walter, and John. Now, am I going to have to say good-bye to Minnie and …maybe James and the others? Do I have to keep waving as they drive off with a new mother and a new father and even sisters and brothers… when I don't have that? It's not fair. I want justice!"

Mrs. Young took a handkerchief which had been tucked into the cuff of her sleeve and she started to wipe the garden dirt from Daisy's face.

Mrs. Young continued, "You need to realize, Daisy, that God has commanded us all to do what is good. You just fed the chickens because you are thoughtful and responsible. God asks us to seek justice and you demonstrate that by always doing your school work. We have many portfolios which show all the wonderful creative school work you have done while you have been here at the Bide-A-While home."

Daisy replied, "Miss Smithy said I can give my portfolios to my new family, so they can see how smart I've been."

Mrs. Young nodded, "Yes. It is your work and it will help your new family get to know you as you have been growing up." She sighed, "As I said earlier, all wars were supposed to end with the last Great War, but wicked hearts which hunger for power have kicked up the dust of turmoil, once again. So, it is Bide-A-While's job to be very careful to place you properly. God asks us to defend the rights of the fatherless and I want to make sure you get the perfect match."

Daisy asked, "Is that something from Isaiah 1:17?"

Mrs. Young smiled. "Yes. See? You have many talents. You obviously study and are a good student. You cannot give up, Daisy. God is preparing just the right home for you."

"With a mother and father and sisters and brothers?" Daisy asked.

"I do not know the specifics of God's plan for you, Daisy. But I do know God is working very hard to arrange things so that you are in the perfect family which will be right for you... Jeremiah 29:11

says that God knows the plans he has for you… *'plans to prosper you and not to harm you… plans to give you hope and a future.'* Here, let me write that down so you remember it."

Mrs. Young crossed the room to a desk, took out a paper, and dipped her pen nib into the inkwell. She quickly wrote the verse, clinking her pen into the glass inkwell as the nib ran dry.

Mrs. Young added, "I'm also jotting down 1Thessalonians 5:18, which says *'give thanks in all circumstances; for this is God's will for you in Christ Jesus.'*"

"Two verses?" Daisy asked.

"And I want you to read them right before we open the doors and when you go to bed to remember that God has a lot of work to do in the background to provide you with the perfect situation."

Daisy replied, "I have been saying my prayers. I already have memorized James 1:5, *'If any of you lacks wisdom, you should ask God, who gives generously to all without finding fault, and it will be given to you.'"*

"See?" Mrs. Young smiled, "You are already speaking with wisdom. Focus on the blessings God has given you. I know you already know Proverbs 3:5 and 6."

Daisy shrugged sheepishly, "I don't have that one memorized, but I do know that it basically says when things get confusing, I need to trust God because he knows more than I do and if I pray and read the scriptures then He will make my path clear, step-by-step..."

"I think that is a fine interpretation," Mrs. Young enthused as she pressed the freshly penned verses into Daisy's hand. "Now, take a look in the mirror and tell yourself that God has a plan for you and you will enjoy visiting with the grown-ups today."

Daisy did just that.

With some time to spare before the doors opened, Daisy slipped into the library and looked up her portfolios to glance through them. She saw her first paper cut out turkey she made for a Thanksgiving. Her finger ran down the notes of her growth both physically and educationally. How she graduated from a four-sided crib to a three-sided bed and then to a regular bed.

The portfolios were also viewed by the school's Trustees. These Trustees were Representatives of Governing Agencies, visiting nurses, and doctors, all God-fearing, who wanted garden parties, picnics, Bible-story-time, and sing-alongs. They wanted to see these cheerful children shine.

She saw notes made by the etiquette teacher who taught manners, sewing, floral arranging, cleaning and how to use real china dishes.

Daisy caught her reflection in a display case in the library and wondered, was she not pretty enough to be adopted or was the delay in getting a family caused because God had to arrange something very particular to suit Daisy. Was it her nose and messy hair ...or was it because God was working out a wonderful plan for her future?

Daisy recalled the day when she ran off to look for Miss Smithy and asked her advice about making better hair.

Miss Smithy had given her some rags and showed Daisy how to roll her hair in strips of cloth, and then tie the ends into a knot.

One day, Daisy tried rolling her hair in rags on her own. It was difficult to sleep on the lumpy rag curlers, but Daisy was sure the results would be worth it.

The results the next morning had made her hair look even worse. The middle of her hair was all frizzy, while the ends stuck out in sharp points.

She had been so upset. Miss Smithy had taken her aside and put her hair into pin curls for the day to fix the mishap.

"Remember you can learn anything," Miss Smithy would remind Daisy, "If you practice. All you need is experience and practice."

Miss Smithy always knew how to comfort the boys and girls at Bide-A-While.

Daisy stood up. She pondered the seasons. Winter days brought hot soup for dinner, thick damp heavy snowfalls, and cold which bit her fingers and toes. Winter would be replaced by Spring.

Spring would bring cool misty mornings and fragile sunny days. Then, Spring would succumb to yet another season, Summer...then Autumn, and so on.

Daisy realized she was simply in a season of time. Sure, the Bide-A-While babies may have been adopted by families before she was, but Daisy was now confident that she would get her own mother and father, just as she had seen the families in the magazines.

And, of course, Daisy's pretty maybe-mother would be married to Daisy's smart maybe-father. Daisy's maybe-father would help set up tents on camping trips, and start fires to roast marshmallows by a lake, where he could teach her to fish, just like the picture on page 43 of that magazine over there.

And then her maybe-parents would tuck Daisy in and kiss her goodnight on the forehead before they would tip-toe out. Getting tucked into her own bed at night was the most important requirement of all.

"God will take care of me," Daisy boldly announced aloud in the empty library. She then marched out of the library and joined the other children just as the doors were opening to let the grown-ups in. Today would be a great Company Day.

3 CHAPTER

As the grown-ups were leaving, Daisy could smell a delicious stew cooking in the kitchen with fragrant aromas wafting throughout the building.

Daisy did not quite connect with a family today. There was always next month.

Then, a woman approached Daisy with Mrs. Young.

"Daisy," Mrs. Young introduced, "This is Mrs. Rosten from the Ladies' Sunshine Club."

Daisy curtseyed politely.

Mrs. Rosten explained to Daisy, "We meet here twice a year and I was the lucky winner who drew your name, Daisy. It is nice to meet you."

"Drew my name?" Daisy asked confused.

Mrs. Rosten enthused, "We put all the orphan names into a basket and one of us picks a name, so we can be your Season Clothing Sponsor. I am happy to announce that I want to take you shopping."

"Do you want a child living in your home?" Daisy asked, wondering if this woman was married or widowed. "Is your husband a soldier in the war?"

Mrs. Rosten smiled and replied, "I have six children of my own. My husband is not a soldier. He is a doctor and he is a very nice man and he loves this Season Clothing Sponsor idea."

"Six children?" Daisy replied, "You must have a very large house."

"Not so large. Each child has a roommate. I asked my sixteen-year-old, Becky, if she had any hand-me-downs to donate to you. But, she said we should take you shopping for something new."

Mrs. Young added, "She wants to be your Season Clothing Sponsor and provide you with a new outfit before our next Company Day, Daisy. Isn't that nice?"

Daisy smiled and curtseyed, "Yes. Thank you for offering to take me shopping. Thank you for explaining that you are not my forever home."

Mrs. Young carefully guided Daisy away from Mrs. Rosten and whispered, "Daisy, Mrs. Rosten is donating her time and money to get you some new clothes. Now we do have a potential match for you, but there was an urgent work emergency and they could not make it today, but they do want to see you. We will set up something at another time for you to meet together."

"A forever family? A pretty mother and a camping father?" Daisy clarified.

Mrs. Young whispered to Daisy, "Let us not confine God to our idea of what we need. Let us trust God. He knows what is best..."

"But Mrs. Rosten has too many children to take me in. She said she will just take me shopping, not adopt me."

Mrs. Young explained, "As far as interviewing your future family, my team needs to first inspect the home to ensure it is suitable for you. The family I have in mind lives far away. We need to make sure it is Godly, safe, and nurturing."

"But if it works out, I can go see the new family? Next weekend?" Daisy asked.

Mrs. Young replied, "If it works out, the family will come here to Bide-A-While for visits. Because they live so far away, you will only visit the family home when it seems certain you will be adopted. In the meantime, be patient and polite to Mrs. Rosten and her teenage daughter Becky."

4 CHAPTER

Becky Rosten, Mrs. Rosten's teenage daughter, had taken up a collection from the allowances of all her siblings. Naturally, Dr. and Mrs. Rosten had added some money to that which their children already donated.

"Hi Daisy," Becky chirped, "Mom said I could take you shopping, so we are going to take the bus to the Dreamland Children's Shoppe. Have you ever been there?"

"I've never really been shopping for clothes for myself..." Daisy shyly admitted.

Becky Rosten grabbed Daisy's hand with a smile and said, "Great. It'll be a fun new adventure, then."

When they arrived, Becky marched straight to the department for girls clothing. Daisy was so excited she thought her heart would beat to bursting!

While Daisy was looking up and around at all the fun decorations, Becky was searching through the racks of options in Daisy's size. Becky had asked what color Daisy liked. What fabric feel does she like. Does she like bows and lace or would she rather something simple where she can play in it and wear it every day.

Daisy was amazed to be having this conversation. She answered all the questions and wondered if she would return to Bide-A-While with an outfit like one of the little girls she had seen in one of the many old donated magazines at Bide-A-While.

"Daisy," announced Becky, "here is just the dress for you!"

Daisy ran to Becky and found her holding up a bright red velvet dress with a square neck, trimmed with white lace over a smooth top and flaring out at the bottom in a swingy full skirt.

Daisy had always been given clothes that, somehow, were bleached to a faded blue or faint pink. But, as she gazed at this dress, she couldn't breathe! Red! Plush red velvet and white lace! She gently touched one sleeve. She had never felt any fabric so soft.

"May I really have it?" Daisy whispered.

"Of course!" said Becky, delighted.

If Becky could have found stockings and ribbons of the same bright red, she would gladly have bought them, as well. Becky found a large white satin hair bow which clipped on with a bright, brass clasp.

Then, Daisy spotted a deep red ribbon displayed on a counter. She pointed and tapped Becky's arm.

Becky looked at the price of the red ribbon, counted her money, then said, "We can get the red ribbon, as well, Daisy!"

Becky also bought Daisy a pair of shiny black patent leather shoes and a pair of socks with white ruffles at the ankle. She finished off the outfit with a little black patent leather purse and put a quarter into it for good luck.

Yes, Daisy and Becky Rosten were both very satisfied with these purchases.

At lunch-time, Becky took Daisy to the Olde Tyme Soda Bar. She checked her finances and saw there was precisely enough money for two big malted shakes with three scoops of ice-cream in each, and a just-enough tip for the waitress.

Mother Rosten, in her car, picked the girls up at two o'clock and Daisy was returned to the Bide-a-While Home. Daisy was tired but happily content, with the joy of that day locked so fast in her memory, that it would last forever while she was on earth and maybe even in Heaven.

After Mrs. Rosten parked in front of the Bide-A-While entrance, Daisy got out of the car, carefully holding the box of beautiful new clothes Becky Rosten had picked out for her. Then Daisy turned to wave at Becky and Mrs. Rosten, who rolled down the window of her car.

"Now, Daisy," Mrs. Rosten explained, "I understand Bide-A-While will soon be presenting a choir performance in the near future, and that you will be in it. We would like to attend. Also, if you do get adopted, you have our address and we would love to get a Christmas card from you and keep in touch."

"Keep in touch? Like friends?" Daisy gasped.

Becky leaned forward to call out the Window.

"That's right, Daisy, like a little sister or something. Write us and let us know how you are."

Miss Smithy spied Daisy being dropped off and was just coming down the steps to meet her. She also waved at Mrs. Rosten, and her daughter Becky.

Mrs. Rosten waved at Miss Smithy and then said to Daisy, "Becky enjoyed shopping with you. Our family is already planning to attend any plays or concerts given at Bide-A-While."

"Thank you again, Becky and Mrs. Rosten," Daisy chirped.

The car crunched gravel beneath its wheels as the Rostens drove away. Daisy stood with Miss Smithy and waved.

5 CHAPTER

Bide-A-While's formal school year was nearly over. The big day before summer vacation was only hours away. On this final day, each child took part in a performance to which the Trustees, employees, volunteers at the orphanage, and their friends, were all invited.

Earlier in the week, they had already begun practicing proper comportment. At each rehearsal assembly, everyone dressed up in their Sunday best clothes. All the children worked hard at being well-mannered as they welcomed visitors.

There had been many days of instruction.

Mrs. Young called speaking properly "elocution," and said every child needed to pronounce each word properly to be successful.

Daisy was assigned to memorize and then present the 23rd Psalm all by herself on stage.

Daisy was terrified, but Mrs. Young reminded Daisy that, "we are born to sing God's praises," so Daisy agreed to try her very best.

She had never performed by herself before, but as Miss Smithy said, "experience is a little learning and a lot of practice".

So, Daisy began to practice.

And, finally one month later, Company Day arrived.

The gardener and his helpers had done a wonderful job around the grounds. The big Assembly Hall was decorated with flowers, leafy branches, paper ribbons and samples of student work. The children were dressed in their finest.

Daisy wore her bright red velvet dress. She felt all aglow inside and knew she just sparkled outside. She stood backstage with her classmates, and every few minutes quickly peeked through the heavy, musty green stage curtains out at the gathering audience.

So many people! Many more visitors were here than she had ever remembered.

Daisy popped her head between two curtain panels, wrapping the velvet curtains around her neck to hide her body. She wanted to see if she recognized anybody in the assembly.

All the seats were full. Suddenly, Daisy spotted Mrs. Rosten and all her children. There was Dr. Rosten, also.

Daisy stuck her hand out to get their attention. It was Becky who noticed Daisy and tapped her mother on the shoulder to wave back. Becky beamed when she noticed Daisy was wearing the new red velvet dress they had purchased together.

Then, Mrs. Young tapped Daisy on the shoulder.

"Daisy," Mrs. Young started, "After the performance this evening, I'd like you to meet somebody."

"Is it Mrs. Rosten and her family? I saw them. I was just waving at them."

Mrs. Young smiled, "Of course you can say hello to the Rostens, but I want you to meet somebody else. No time now... Just look for me as soon as the final curtain call... It's performance-time!"

Before Daisy could respond, she saw the curtain was already opening up and she needed to get off the stage.

Daisy wondered... Oh the idea was too thrilling! She closed her eyes, shutting out everything around her so she could think the thought completely. So many people were sitting out in that huge audience that there might... there just might even be a mother out there! A mother just for her! A mother! A mother! A MOTHER!

The merry audience thundered its opening applause and the delightful program started out with the babies singing.

The audience responded with plenty of "Ahs!" and "Ohs!" and clapping.

Next, the children in the primary grades put on a play which finished to loud and enthusiastic applause.

Several more presentations were met with joyfully noisy audience enthusiasm.

And now it was Daisy's turn.

Mrs. Young motioned to Daisy, beckoning her to get on stage. Daisy hesitated, but Mrs. Young gave her a gentle shove and there was no turning back. Everyone was watching.

Everyone.

Daisy began:

*"The Lord is my mother.
I shall not want."*

Daisy was aware of the ripple of laughter that rolled through the Hall. Daisy, shut her eyes, and continued as she had practiced, not daring to stop.

*"...lets me lie down in green pastures...
...leads me beside still waters,
...restores my soul.
...leads me in the paths of righteousness for His Name's sake...
Yea, though I walk through the Valley...
I will fear no evil, for Thou art with me.
Thy rod and Thy staff they comfort me...
You set a table for me
   in the presence of mine enemies.
You anoint my head with oil. My cup runs over.
Surely goodness and mercy shall follow me*

All the days of my life, And I will dwell in the house of God forever..."

When she ended, she felt weak and very thirsty, but Mrs. Young patted Daisy's hand and said she had done a fine job.

After all the children had performed, they came back on stage, holding hands for a final bow. The curtain closed and then they all rushed to join the audience in the reception hall for refreshments.

Daisy, however, turned away and started off to help Miss Smithy with the babies. She did not notice the young lady who was walking toward Mrs. Young's Office.

Before reaching the babies area, Daisy stopped at the noisy reception hall crowded with grown-up visitors and nicely dressed, very polite orphans.

Mrs. Young approached Daisy with the pretty lady in tow. Daisy, suddenly unable to swallow, felt her heart begin to thump with a mix of hope and apprehension.

"Someone has asked about you, Daisy," Mrs. Young said, "Someone who would like to be responsible for you."

"Is this my new mother?" Daisy asked.

The woman smiled and said, "Mrs. Young showed me all your portfolios... I feel as if I know you quite well."

"My portfolios? In the library?" Daisy asked. Mrs. Young nodded.

The woman continued, "Daisy, Mrs. Young's team spent a lot of time visiting with me frequently at my home. Then, today she said, if you wish, I can come and visit you right here, even when it is not Company Day."

Daisy was so overcome with joy, she jumped into Mrs. Young's arms and squeezed her very tightly, "I have a match! You matched me with a mother!"

Minnie spotted Daisy in the crowded reception hall. Minnie turned to speak to her newly adopted family and explained Daisy's situation.

As Mrs. Young returned Daisy's happy hugs, she laughed and said, "It's days like this that make me love my job."

Daisy excitedly asked the pretty woman, "Does your husband like camping? Oh, I want to learn to fish, and build a fire, and the stars...I want to learn about the stars in the sky..." Daisy took a breath and added, "How many visits until I can go home with you, Mother?"

Mrs. Young interrupted Daisy. "Daisy, your new mother is not married. There is no husband. No Dad."

Daisy stopped a bit. After a long moment, she asked, "Can she take care of me?"

"Yes," the maybe-Mother replied. "I have a very good job...."

Mrs. Young added, "And she has live-in help at home."

Daisy became very quiet. "I was praying for a mother... and father."

"Daisy, this lady wants to be responsible for you, but you are the one who needs to make the final decision. Let me know how to note the Bide-A-While Children's Log Book. It is entirely up to you, Daisy."

Heart pounding, Daisy nodded, "Okay. Gosh..."

Mrs. Young said, "I know it is noisy here in this crowded reception hall. Why not use my office for a few minutes? It's right over there. Have a chat... I'll return in a minute with some tea."

In Mrs. Young's office, Daisy's maybe-new-mother offered a seat to Daisy and then sat down herself. Mrs. Young closed the door as she left. The celebratory crowd in the reception hall was louder than ever.

As they waited for Mrs. Young to return, the maybe-mother said, "Daisy, I'm sure you have some questions for me... Do you like cake with tea?"

Daisy saw her portfolios had been placed on the table. This maybe-mother had already seen all of Daisy's reports about how she was growing up. But Daisy did not know anything about the lady.

The pretty maybe-mother smiled and tapped the portfolios, "I've already gotten a chance to read about you and loved what I saw. I had been praying for a little girl with your unique blend of talents and personality, and I thank God I finally found you. But, you may not know much about me, so ask me anything you like…"

Daisy smiled, took a breath, and the two started to talk.

6 CHAPTER

"How did your time with the pretty maybe-mother go, Daisy? My new-mom said she thinks your maybe-mother drove a long way to come visit you here," Minnie said, as she took a damp rag to wipe up the last table in the now empty reception hall.

"My maybe-mother is very nice," Daisy replied. "While we were all talking in the office, Mrs. Young explained to me that my maybe-mother is a stat...statis...statistician."

"A what?" asked Minnie.

"She does math and science at the government information office. She worked really, really hard to get the highest education that exists! And then she became a scientist... statis... statistician."

"Oh, my..." Minnie exclaimed, amazed.

Daisy added, "Then my maybe-mother said to Mrs. Young that when she was a child, her own family was so kind and helpful when she was growing up and wanted to be a scientist. Then my maybe-mother said now that she's a grown-up she wants to be a kind and helpful family to someone who is growing up right now. Maybe that will be me."

After a moment, Minnie asked, "What's the maybe-Dad like?"

Daisy took a deep breath, then quietly announced, "Mrs. Young said there's no maybe-Dad."

"No Dad?" marveled Minnie. "Why?"

Daisy shrugged. "Mrs. Young said my maybe-mother worked so hard to get educated and become a scientist, she didn't have time to look for a Dad for me."

"Oh, my…" Minnie whispered, amazed. "Your maybe-mother is so pretty, and she's so smart. What do you think about being adopted by her?"

"Great!" Daisy said, "I did not imagine things this way, but she is somebody I wish I could be like when I grow up. How did your weekend go with your maybe-family, Minnie?"

Minnie was finishing up the final bit of her after-dinner-chores as she chatted with Daisy. Minnie tossed the cleaning-rag into the laundry bin and then meandered with Daisy to join the other children in the Bide-A-While recreation room.

Minnie shared, "I think my maybe-family liked me. It's nice I can spend the night with them because they live close now, but they said they may move."

"Move? Where?" Daisy asked.

Minnie replied, "Closer to where your maybe-mother lives, Daisy. Far away from here." Minnie clapped her hands together with a fresh idea, "Wouldn't it be grand, Daisy, if, when we're adopted, we ended up at the same school?"

Daisy asked Minnie, "Does that mean you'll leave Bide-A-While, Minnie?"

Minnie and Daisy sat at one of the book tables near where the smaller children were playing with blocks.

Minnie looked at Daisy and said, "I told my maybe-family that I like cats and they said they don't have pets. If they ever got one, they would get a cat. So, I hope I'll leave Bide-A-While and be part of their family soon. Do you think you'd be ready to leave Bide-A-While?"

"Leave?" Daisy wondered.

Bide-A-While was Daisy's home. This is what she was used to. Could she feel comfortable in a new living situation? Even with a nice maybe-mother?

"Well," Minnie said while opening up a picture book and flipping through the pages, "You don't have to decide until tomorrow. That's when Mrs. Young is going to work everything out with your new maybe-mother."

"How do you know?" Daisy asked.

"Because you came back late. I was in the dining hall setting the tables for dinner. You went to get washed up. After your new maybe-mother dropped you off, she spoke with Mrs. Young in her office. I overheard…"

"What? Did my maybe-mother ask for me to visit her home? Or Adopt me?" Daisy's eyes opened wide.

"I didn't hear everything…" Minnie said nodding. "But, I think it will be up to you tomorrow to decide if you want her to be your mother or not. She likes you, so now you have to tell Mrs. Young if your name should be written in the Bide-A-While Children's Log Book as having been matched with a family or not."

Daisy had a lot to think about.

7 CHAPTER

Daisy had never been away from the Bide-a-While for more than one day. She packed her mother-portfolio, her nighty, six pairs of socks, five hair ribbons, two pairs of play shorts and one shirt.

When maybe-Mother, as Daisy now thought of her, came for her on that sizzling bright summer afternoon, Daisy was wearing her heavy red velvet dress. Beads of sweat sat on Daisy's brow and trickled down her back.

"Aren't you warm?" Mother asked, concerned. Daisy nodded that she was.

Mother smiled, uncertain.

Daisy said goodbye to her friends and Miss Smithy and Mrs. Young and Cook. She felt awkward as she walked stiffly toward the main gate and out to her new Mother's car.

Mother had met two of Daisy's dream requirements. She was pretty. And she was a "car mother" like Mrs. Rosten.

It was a long drive to Mother's home. Daisy wanted to remember every leaf on each tree they passed as they drove away along the road. She was heading to Mother's home, Daisy's new home…

When they arrived at Mother's house, Daisy gasped. It matched her dream, too! It was perfect. Just perfect!

"Mother, will you get married so I can have a father?" Daisy asked.

Mother sighed, "I've been working at the statistics bureau for the war effort, Daisy, and it has taken up most of my time. When I asked God for my path, he led me to you. I do have help at home, so when I am tied up at work, there will always be somebody here to be part of your family. I know it is not what you imagined... but..."

"I think this is a very good match, Mother. Please do not worry. This is perfect...for me. God set this all up just for me and I'm glad you are part of this. It's okay that you are a Miss instead of a Missus."

Mother hugged Daisy.

"Maybe we can bake cookies together?" Daisy suggested.

"Oh, well," Mother replied, "Mrs. Abbott is a better cook than I am."

Daisy nodded as they got out of the car, "It's OK. I don't need a kitchen mother. You are a car mother. That is perfect for me."

Daisy could tell that her kind words to this new Mother were taken appreciatively.

As they entered the house, Daisy saw a man and a woman. The man was dressed like a butler, and the woman was dressed as a lady's maid.

"These two very nice people are my helpers," Mother whispered to Daisy.

Daisy had seen pictures of people in those outfits in the magazines at Bide-A-While. She thought they may be called uniforms. Both of them were very professional, a bit distant, but nice enough.

"Let me give you a tour of your new home," Mother shared. "First, this is Mr. and Mrs. Abbott."

Daisy curtseyed.

On the tour, Mother showed Daisy the library, which had so very many shelves of books. In the corner was an old writing desk, which Mother explained she used when she was a child and did all her homework on it. Next came the kitchen, the backyard, the victory garden, where vegetables were grown, then the formal living room and finally the dining room.

Mr. and Mrs. Abbott had prepared a lovely meal in anticipation of this arrival. Mother showed Daisy where to sit, and then Mr. and Mrs. Abbott served them.

At first, conversation was a bit awkward. Daisy didn't know how to converse around "staff" or how to address them.

Daisy was most careful to be polite, and soon found that this mother did have something Daisy had never thought about. This mother listened carefully to everything Daisy said, as if what Daisy felt and thought were extremely important.

The moon eased up into night's soft black sky and Daisy could see it through the branches of a great oak tree outside the dining-room window.

Daisy stifled a yawn.

After dessert, Mother gently guided Daisy upstairs to a room newly painted white and pink with wallpaper sprinkled all over with tiny rosebuds.

"I hope you like it, Daisy," she said. She waited at the door as Daisy walked in. "Through there," she said, pointing to an archway, "is your very own bathroom... And when I was your age, I had a room like this. There are lots of books for you to read. And you can have my doll collection. I loved to play with them when I was your age. Or we can get others if you like."

Daisy's mouth opened, but she was so amazed, not one word could come out. Books everywhere! And dolls! Baby dolls! Elegant dolls! Beautiful, happy, large, small, more shapes and sizes than she had ever imagined could exist!

"Now when you're ready to go to bed, just remember to turn off the lights. You can stay up as long as you like. This is vacation time." Mother paused, uncertain how to say good-night to Daisy. "Good-night, Daisy. I'm... I'm so very happy you are here..."

The door closed softly. Daisy heard Mother's footsteps fade as she moved off down the hall.

Tears stung Daisy's eyes.

And then, as quickly as they came, she brushed them away.

Of course, thought Daisy! Mother just left because she doesn't know about tucking-in, saying night-prayers, and kissing foreheads good-night. Why, she doesn't know much at all about how a mother should act. She has never been a mother! She has no experience!

Daisy had to help. But how?

She turned the problem over and over in her mind as she carefully explored the room. She examined the books and handled each doll lovingly. But her deep down thoughts still worried about her new mother.

Soon Daisy could not keep her eyes from closing, and her head from nodding. She decided she had better say her own night prayers before she settled down to play.

After she whispered her quiet prayers, she dragged several books and dolls up onto the bed. She would wash up and change into her nightgown just as soon as...

Daisy drifted off to sleep.

The next morning, Daisy awoke to the sound of birds singing right outside her window. She gasped when she realized she had slept in her red velvet dress all night.

Carefully, she hung it up. Oh, it had become all wrinkled and creased! She tried to smooth out the worst of it, then raced to wash up and put on her play clothes.

As she hurried, she wondered what she could do about the fact that this mother, poor thing, wasn't used to mothering. She thought about the mother's gentle smile, and worried eyes, and felt a pang of pity.

And then, in an instant, she found a solution to the problem.

She quickly made her bed, trying to get all the fancy pillows back in their right places, picked up her portfolio, and tip-toed downstairs.

The mother was waiting for her and turned as she heard Daisy enter the huge living room. She gave Daisy that wonderful warm smile of greeting.

"Ready for breakfast?" Mother asked.

"Yes," Daisy answered softly, as she climbed onto the sofa, "but could we sit here for a little while, first?"

"Of course," said Mother, folding her hands in her lap as she sat beside the little girl.

"I know why you don't know how a mother acts..." Daisy began to explain.

Mother's eyes grew wide, then very sad. Daisy felt awful when she saw what her words had done.

Daisy hurried to add, "You don't know how a mother acts because you have no experience... And experience is a little learning and a lot of practice."

She opened her portfolio of magazine clippings and began turning the pages, looking up at Mother from time to time to make sure she wasn't turning them too fast.

On one page, there was a picture of a mother hugging a child. "The little girl has just come home from school," Daisy explained. "See? She has a new school bag. I know this picture is advertising soup, but this is a good example of what a mother can do with her daughter. Eat soup together and then hug."

Next, there was a mother baking a special cake in the kitchen with her child helping. On another page, there was a mother bike-riding with her daughter.

The next magazine picture showed a healthy family jogging along a country road. The smiling mother was on one side of the picture, and the smiling father on the other side. Three children, all safe and happy, jogged in between the parents.

The next image showed a "picnic" mother. After that picture, there was a "bed-time stories" mother. Then there was...

"Oh, Daisy..." said Mother, looking down at the portfolio held by Daisy. Her voice seemed small and choked. "I'm not... I'm not a mom who cooks and sews. Moms who cook and sew are wonderful moms. But that's not me... That's not what I ever wanted to do... I'm a statistician."

Now it was Daisy's eyes which grew wide. "I know, but what is that, really?"

"It's a kind of math," Mother explained.

"Oh, I'm very good at math," Daisy assured her.

"I know, darling…" and then Mother stopped speaking. She sat quietly for a long moment, as Daisy waited.

Then Mother continued, "It's a wonderful job that I do. I work in the city. In a huge office building. Writing reports. That's what I really do."

"Reports?" Daisy asked.

"Studies… about why people do what they do…go where they go…buy what they buy… and what they are likely to be doing in the next ten years… and I…" Her voice broke again, and her words were so quiet now that Daisy had to lean forward to hear them.

"I wanted to help..."

Mother suddenly got up and hurried into the study way at the other side of the living room. The door closed behind her, but its latch did not click, and as Daisy watched, the door drifted opened again, just a very little bit. Daisy sat still, not knowing quite what to do.

After a long silence, Daisy heard Mother's words, soft and gentle.

"... dear God, I thought adoption would demonstrate my benevolent generosity during the war, but this child has affected me in a way I had not anticipated. Dear Savior, please make me worthy to be this little girl's mother. I thought I was doing something for You... but You are doing so much more for me...through this child...Help me to be the mother You want me to be... the mother she wants me to me..."

She's a "praying mother" too, Daisy realized. *We can pray together.*

When Mother came back, she sat beside Daisy again and nodded at the portfolio which still lay opened on Daisy's lap.

"I will study your book, Daisy," Mother said, smiling softly. "And I am sure I can learn how to be a wonderful mother. This collection of magazine clippings tells me you put a lot of thought into this. I may not be the mothers in these pictures, but we can try these activities together and learn together. Would you like that?"

Daisy looked at Mother and suddenly felt herself filling up with the kind of heavenly love that only God can put into the heart of a child. How Daisy wanted to protect this mother! Her Mother.

"You don't have to copy any of the pictures I showed you," said Daisy. "You are the perfect Mother for me. And together, Mother and daughter, we are the perfect family."

THE END

ABOUT THE AUTHORS

Wynter Sommers is the pseudonym for an American writing team. One is a technology specialist. The other has thirty years of experience applying her PhD in Education to lovingly teach classrooms of enthusiastic students. Both have a heart to inspire creativity in children, encourage supportive family bonds, and share life as it was in America during WWII.

Wynter Sommers hopes you enjoy the other **Daisy's Adventures** stories in this series.

www.ingramcontent.com/pod-product-compliance
Lightning Source LLC
Chambersburg PA
CBHW031226170426
43191CB00030B/294